Inner Journey Meditations

First published by Asherah Books, 2018

Design: Editorial Kier

A CIP catalogue record for this book is available from the British Library.

Paperback ISBN 978-1-909187-94-8

Ebook ISBN 978-1-909187-95-5

CHER CHEVALIER & LIZ SOLARI

Inner Journey Meditations

Asherah Books
London

Contents

Introduction

Cher Chevalier is world-renowned Spiritual Adviser, Co-creator of The #HANDSOFF Campaign, Founder and CEO of Animals Actually Ltd, and Author of the following 30 books: The Hidden Secrets of a Modern Seer, The Hidden Truths of a Modern Seer, The Hidden Life of a Modern Seer, SLIM: Step Lightly In Mind, Body, Spirit, and ANIMALS ACTUALLY A - Z for children. Cher endured near death experiences in childhood, after which her psychic and mystical experiences began. Cher has worked as a Spiritual Adviser for over 20 years and leads a devotional life.

Liz Solari is an Argentine actress, activist for animal rights and Unicef Ambassador. Her spiritual awakening came in 2010 after she experienced the death of a loved one. That same year, Liz met her spiritual teacher, Cher Chevalier, and her training in meditation practices began. In 2017 she created Inner Journey with Liz Solari, a YouTube channel that inspires others to meditate and live in harmony with all beings.

Cher and Liz collaborated on this Inner Journey Meditations project to share their deep respect for meditation practices with the rest of the world. It is their wish that Cher's meditations coupled with Liz's videos will help to manifest the Divine Plan for a heavenly earth.

"May all the meditations in this little book assist and uplift all beings on their evolutionary journey to The Divine."

Love and blessings,
Cher & Liz

www.spiritualadviser.co.uk
www.lizsolari.com

CHAPTER 1

Forgiveness Meditations

11

Forgiveness of Others

Find somewhere to sit that is quiet and comfortable.
Close your eyes. Have your hands loosely in your lap.

Breathe gently and deeply.

Focus on all the beings that you need to forgive.

Picture them one at a time in your mind.

Ask each of them to forgive you. And wait patiently until
you feel good energy between you and them.

Take your time.

Close this meditation with a prayer of thanks to God.

Open your eyes when you are ready.

13

Forgiveness of Self

Find somewhere to sit that is peaceful and comfortable. Close your eyes and have your hands loosely in your lap. Breathe gently and deeply.

Focus on all the things that you need to forgive yourself for.

Be honest and truthful with yourself. This is between you and God only.

As you forgive yourself for each thing, wait calmly until any feeling of guilt or shame is transmuted. And until you feel love for yourself.

Take your time.

Close this meditation with a prayer of love for God.

Open your eyes when you are ready.

Forgiveness from God

Find a private place to sit where you won't be disturbed. Close your eyes. Have your hands loosely in your lap. Breathe gently and deeply.

Focus on all the beings that you have hurt with your words or your actions.

Picture them one at a time in your mind.

Humbly ask God to forgive you and to reveal how you may atone to bring about harmony between yourself and those you have hurt.

Take your time.

Close this meditation with your commitment to show mercy to others.

Open your eyes when you are ready.

17

CHAPTER 2

Gratitude Meditations

19

Gratitude for Everything

Find somewhere soft to lie down.

Close your eyes. Rest your hands gently on your chest.

Breathe slowly and deeply.

Focus on everything and everyone that you are grateful for.

Picture all of them clearly, and feel the joy in your heart as you meditate on them one by one.

Allow yourself to be supremely happy. There are no limits.

Close this meditation in the blissful presence of God.

Smile.

Then open your eyes.

Gratitude for Parents

Find somewhere cosy to sit down.

Close your eyes. Rest your hands gently in your lap.

Lift your mind to consider the glory of creation.

Focus on your parents, those beings who brought you into manifestation.

You have come into this realm through them.

Recognise the meaning of this deeply. And with gratitude, bless your parents for this grand opportunity.

Meditate on the infinite possibilities for your life.

Allow yourself to be supremely optimistic. You have no limits.

Close this meditation in gratitude to your Divine Mother and Heavenly Father.

Shine inwardly with positive power.

Open your eyes.

Gratitude to God

Find the place where you feel most inspired.

Close your eyes. Journey inwards to your inner sanctuary.

Feel your levels of joy rise.

Focus on all the things that you are grateful to God for: every breath, each blessing, all experiences of real love, the miracle that is your life.

Be grateful to your Divine creator and show it - dance, sing, laugh, feel joy in your spirit and every fibre of your being, then offer it to God as a token of your gratitude.

Abandon negativity, pledge to complain no more. Allow yourself to be grateful beyond measure and bask in the lofty heights of happiness.

Close this meditation in the loving presence of God.

Gratefully embrace your inner divinity.

Then open your eyes.

CHAPTER 3

Love
Meditations

27

Love of Others

Breathe and realise that you are breathing the same air as all other beings.

Recognise that we all have the same needs, humans as well as animals. We all need to breathe, eat and have shelter.

Feel your love for others grow as you notice that our needs make us one.

Focus on all beings having their needs met, and living in safety and comfort. Our world is a blessing for all beings to experience. Live lovingly and respect the sacredness of all life in its totality.

Love others with your thoughts, words and actions. Wish all others well. Love the earth that is our mutual home. Be caring as you journey through this life. We are all travelling through this world together - let us assist each other along the way.

Abandon judgement, replace it with compassion.

Allow yourself to love others beyond compare and reach the noble shores of harmlessness.

Close this meditation by loving all souls as one.

Tenderly acknowledge our unity.

29

Love of Self

Listen closely to the beat of your heart.

Love yourself with gentleness. Life is a gift, fragile and precious.

Let kindness reign in your thoughts about yourself.

Focus on all the things that you love to do, feel loved in yourself, be loving towards yourself in every moment.

Life is fleeting and each moment that passes cannot be gotten back. Bless yourself.

You are alive now. And you are a miracle.

Your Divine creator has awarded you this unique opportunity - to be you!

Celebrate with joyful jubilation. Pamper yourself, treat yourself. Love yourself beyond the realms of reason and live blissfully.

Bless God for your Divine spark.

This is your life. Love it!

Love of God

Soar in your spirit full of light, and dwell in the love of God. The gates of your heart now open, let heavenly love flow.

Fear and pain cannot reside here, but only love most true and pure. Be enfolded in this love most high, eternally sweet and sublime.

Rest in your love of God. With each breath, cast your every care. Your love of God filling you with peace as you softly declare: "I Love You, God."

Waste no time, love the Divine and declare it from your soul.

Do all for God's love. Make the love of God your goal.

Close this meditation with a commitment to love God, forever.

God is Love.

CHAPTER 4

Peace Meditations

35

Peace with Others

Sit in complete silence.

Close your eyes. Be tranquil.

Free yourself from any disturbance.

Let your mind, your body and your spirit be in total quietude.

Hush yourself into a state of soundless calm. And just be.

Extend this state of peace within you out to all beings and the universe itself.

Know that you can create peace. And share it with others.

Peace is a power, its root is non-violence, its friend is harmony.

Aim to be at peace with all others at all times.

May peace be the guiding light to a smooth and pleasant existence for all.

Be a steward of peace.

Peace with Self

Be hushed. Soundless and still.

Close your eyes. Journey inwards to calm your emotions.

Seek inner balance.

Transmute all agitation. Let peace transform your worries into bliss.

With every breath, create peace. Breathe peace.

Smile gently to yourself until you are engulfed by peace.

Visualise peace guiding all aspects of your life.

Be a guardian of your inner peace and build your own paradise.

Be a creator of peace.

Peace with God

Kneel, humbly and in silence.

Close your eyes. Offer yourself to God.

Be patient.

This noble exercise must be performed with reverence.

From the depths of your heart, pray for the grace to be at peace with God.

Release all anger. Erase all blame. Transmute all guilt and shame.

Forgiving yourself and all others, focus on the path to peace with God.

With admiration and appreciation, bless God for all that is good and peaceful, for every glimpse of peace you have been blessed to enjoy.

Esteem your Divine creator and the power that is peace.

Respectfully request that you may be approved to enter into the peace of God. Acknowledge this opportunity to claim the greatest treasure - peace with God.

"In contemplation may
we find peace"

CHAPTER 5

Faith Meditations

45

Faith in Others

Open your mind to life's infinite possibilities.

Trust that every being has its own unique journey.

Believe in the potential of others. Seek and nurture the good in others.

Have faith that others all have the capacity for greatness.

Smile as you ponder the wonderful unity of all life.

Visualise the talents of others manifesting to benefit all beings.

See the light in others and build a beautiful world.

Be a beacon of faith.

47

Faith in Self

Tune in and open your mind.

Your spirit is eternal and all knowing. Believe that life holds no limits for you.

You can choose excellence in any given moment. Have faith in your unique capacity for greatness.

Within you lies the seed of perfection.

Tread confidently the path of an exemplary life.

Visualise your gifts manifesting to build a perfect world.

Shine your light of faith.

Faith in God

Your existence is a gift from God.

With all of your heart, mind, body and soul, have faith in God.

Trust in the Divine creator.

Believe that God is supremely good. Be certain that God is the good in all.

Have faith that you were created to glorify your Divine creator.

Be in awe and praise of all that is beautiful, good and true.

May pure faith in God exalt and elevate all beings.

Without faith it is impossible to please God.

With faith in God all things are possible, even heaven on earth.

CHAPTER 6

Patience Meditations

53

Patience with Others

Be patient with others.

Wait, without criticism.

Do not push or rush.

Realise that timing is sacred.

Be above anxiety.

Endure and you will procure tranquility.

Let patience reveal its finesse.

Patience with others leads to happiness.

Without force, things grow.

Be patient and observe how life flows.

Patience with Self

Be tolerant with yourself.

Wait, on purpose.

Be guided by intuition, not impulse.

Pause, without pressure.

Be a friend of time, for it is sacred.

Relax and breathe.

Secure for yourself a patient heart.

Let patience be your ally.

Patience with yourself leads to fulfilment.

Let go, and allow life to flow.

Be the most patient person you know.

Patience in God's Timing

God's timing is a treasure beyond measure.

Receive with your spirit its secrets.

Hear the whispers from on high: *"God's timing is perfect. And all things will be in sweet harmony, when all beings come to know."*

Patience in God's timing is a call, to wait for the Divine plan to bless us all.

God's goal is for us to be whole, not just you or me, but everybody, animals and all.

Picture in your mind a world at ease, free from disease, and suffering.

See in your heart that if we all play our part and wait for God's timing, that all will be as God planned it to be - truly heavenly.

Rest in God's timing.

CHAPTER 7

Giving Meditations

61

Giving to Others

As you breathe, you give and receive.

Free your mind from fear and lack.

See that giving is a part of spiritual living.

Enjoy sharing and giving back.

Let your heart urge you to be giving to others.

Bless others with your time and kind words, provide for others needs.

Comfort others with harmless foods and caring actions.

Learn that giving money to meet a need will always be rewarded as a good deed.

Be as generous as you can and give joyfully.

Be a lighthouse in the darkness of others needs.

Be giving to others today.

Giving to Self

Breathe and know that you are you.

You are your constant companion.

You will be with you forever.

Learn to be your own best friend.

Give warmly and freely to yourself all that you may need.

Enjoy nurturing and being with you.

Give to yourself all that is good and healthful.

Bless yourself with time to do all the things you wish to.

Speak kindly words to yourself.

Comfort yourself with harmless foods and caring actions.

Be happy living with a giving attitude.

Be giving to yourself each day.

Giving to God

Be still, and give to God.

Be giving of all that is sweet and pure within you.

Your most loving thoughts.

Your worthy prayers.

Your noblest actions.

Giving to God in such ways is the highest form of praise.

Bless God with your time and kind words of thanks.

Create beautiful gifts to give to God - a poem, a painting, a song.

Learn that giving to God is living honourably.

Look inside you, find what you may give joyfully to God, now.

Enter into a loving and giving relationship with God.

Be giving to God, always.

CHAPTER 8

Responsibility
Meditations

69

Responsibility for Others

Focus on duty - all those you are responsible for.

With clarity, recognise and embrace your role.

Release blame, guilt and fear, and take control.

You have trustworthiness, loyalty and maturity in your soul.

Be confident as you acknowledge your tasks.

Treat and teach children well.

Honour relationships with fidelity.

With respect and morality, proceed.

Bless others with your strength and reliability.

Guide and provide kindly for those in your care.

Comfort them by being there.

Be a safe-haven and the answer to others needs.

Be responsible for others indeed.

Responsibility for Self

Focus on duty - your responsibility for yourself.

With clarity, recognise and welcome your mission.

Release guilt, insecurity and fear.

You have bravery, stability and maturity in your soul.

Be confident you will reach your goal.

Plan and provide for yourself well.

Lead, structure and order well.

Be resolute and unshakeable, and succeed.

Your inner strength will meet your every need.

Grow capable and dependable by the hour.

Governed by your higher power.

Responsibility to God

Focus on your duty to God.

With clarity, recall any and all promises you have made.

Release doubt, fear and selfishness.

You have boldness, faithfulness and Godliness in your spirit.

Be fixed and immovable in your holy tasks.

All beings have a quest, a calling, a vocation.

Pursue this undertaking, and perform your purpose.

Aim with all your might to complete your assignment.

You are able.

Nothing is impossible with God.

Leave no debt behind.

Fulfil your responsibility to God.

"In reflection may
we find wisdom"

CHAPTER 9

Gifts Meditations

79

Gifts of Others

Search in your spirit the manifold gifts that fill the universe.

Each gift utterly unique in its manifestation.

Gifts are bestowed upon all beings.

With wonder, ponder this fact.

Gifts are conferred in many and varied ways.

The gifts of favour that lie in unmissable opportunities.

Talents and flair for creativity.

The gifts of healing touch.

Gifts of humour that uplift humanity.

The gifts of medicine, miracles, and understanding.

Be inspired by all marvellous and magnificent gifts.

The gifts of others are endless.

Gifts of Self

Search within you the manifold gifts with which you are endowed.

Be in awe of your utter uniqueness. With wonder, ponder the exceptional.

Your gifts are dazzling, even in their seed form.

Tend to them all and neglect not.

Nurture and grow them.

Be encouraged that only you can display your gifts as you do.

Develop and promote your gifts with training, education and meditation.

Tap into your well of wonders and allow your gifts to flourish.

Happiness and discipline will unveil your hidden treasures.

Seek the favour of fantastic opportunities.

Nourish your talents and expertise.

Be amazed by all your marvellous and magnificent gifts.

Gifts are miracles waiting to manifest.

Gifts to God

All gifts are from God.

Inherited, bestowed, given and granted to all beings.

Fix your gaze on glory.

Set your sights on and be astonished at eternity.

Use all your gifts to please and deify God.

May the flowering of your gifts be offered to God.

Consecrate your gifts to God with joyfulness.

Never allow pride to rob you of your prize.

Revere and hold most dear your gifts to God.

Adore all the more each moment of golden circumstance.

Sing, dance, create, write, and live your life as a gift to God.

CHAPTER 10

Healing Meditations

87

Healing of Others

Be at ease in your soul. Soften your perspective.

Healing power rises in rest and relaxation.

Attune your mind and spirit and wish others well.

Allow healing thoughts to flow through you to others.

Use all your gifts to relieve distress.

With loving intention send out healing light.

You may heal through your hands, heart, words and mind.

All healing comes from the Divine.

Be a channel for healing rays to shine.

Pray for healing of others.

Healing of Self

Look deep within you.

Resist stress and let healing power flow.

Study your emotions with great care.

Root out all causes of your dis-ease.

Release all fear, envy and anger.

Allow healing light to soothe your entire being.

With loving intention visualise healing light.

Pray for restoration in your soul, body and mind.

All healing comes from the Divine.

Nestle in comforting healing rays.

Pray for healing of self.

Healing the World

Look at the world around you.

See the devastation our earth heaves to bear.

Study the state of our planet with great care.

Your prayers and actions can heal and repair.

Our beautiful world we can cure.

Believe and respond to the urgent call.

Our environment needs to be saved by us all.

Be concerned for the future of your children's home.

Mother earth cannot heal all alone. Humanity must right its wrongs.

Restore the balance for which earth longs.

May humans mend their selfish ways.

Pray for heavenly healing rays.

CHAPTER 11

Karma Meditations

95

Karma of Family

The law of karma applies to us all.

In family groups there is a special call.

All members of your clan agreed to achieve harmony before life began.

You may disagree and even live separately.

Yet love and care must remain.

Be supportive if only in prayer and heart.

Vowing never to abandon your dutiful part.

Karma can punish and be most harsh to correct the pattern of a family path.

Do your utmost to be kind and not harm.

Be at peace with your family.

Forgiveness invites calm.

Karma of Self

Your own karma may be good or bad.

You are the creator of it all.

Master your emotions.

Choose good.

Any debt you may owe in thought word or deed, will surely come back to you indeed.

Be strong and positive.

Know the rules of how you should live.

Negative karma can be transcended.

Follow simple rules.

Be at peace, and do no harm in thought, word or deed.

Learn forgiveness and you will be freed.

Karma of Collective

Supreme goodness lies at the heart of us all.

To see we're all one is the karmic call.

When we harm another we harm ourself.

Karma applies to you and everyone else.

If you wish to be free and happy, wish it for all others and it can be.

Help yourself, others and the world.

Leave a legacy of which you can be proud.

We cannot escape God's perfect laws.

To perfect our ways, God asks of us all.

Be at peace with all beings as your earthly family.

As a collective we can live in harmony.

CHAPTER 12

God's Will
Meditations

103

God's Will for Others

God's Will is perfect for all beings.

Each and everyone is a unique spark of the Divine.

The perfect plan for each being is distinctive.

The choice of free will or God's Will lies with us all.

God's Will leads beings to perfection.

Misuse of free will leads to karmic repercussions.

God's Will is just and true, and the path to emancipation
from suffering.

All can be in God's Will by choosing harmlessness.

All can choose to become Godly.

God's Will for Self

God's Will is perfect and eternal.

You are a unique spark of the Divine.

The perfect plan for you lies in God's Will.

The choice of free will or God's Will is up to you.

Live truthfully and peacefully.

Following God's Will leads to joy.

Misuse of free will creates darkness.

God's Will is just and true, and the path to emancipation for you.

You can be in God's Will by causing no harm.

In God's Will you will become Godly.

God's Will for The World

God's Will for the world is heaven on earth.

As sparks of the Divine we can co-create heaven.

God's Divine Plan is for all beings to be in joy and harmony.

All beings were created to glorify God.

Love and compassion are the highest laws.

Everything we think, eat, do and say must be harmless.

God's Will is for the world to be glorious and good.

This world God created is full of beauty and abundance.

Respect, honour and live in God's Will.

The world is counting on us.

Heaven on earth beckons.

God's Will be done.

"In meditation may
we find our Divinity"

Printed in Great Britain
by Amazon

Inner Journey Meditations

with

CHER CHEVALIER & LIZ SOLARI

Inner Journey Meditations is an inspired work that aims to assist all beings on their journey to the Divine. Cher and Liz collaborated on this project to share their deep respect for the practice of meditation.

Cher Chevalier is a world-renowned spiritual adviser, and author of more than thirty books. Liz Solari is an actress, activist for animal rights and Unicef Ambassador.

ASHERAH BOOKS
LONDON

ISBN 9781909187948

90000

9 781909 187948

ERIN, RODERICK

and

30p
16|6

The

Diffability

Bunch

By Fliss Goldsmith   Illustrated by Ian R. Ward